I0798897

DINOSAUR SCIENCE

WHOSE BUM DID T. REX BITE?

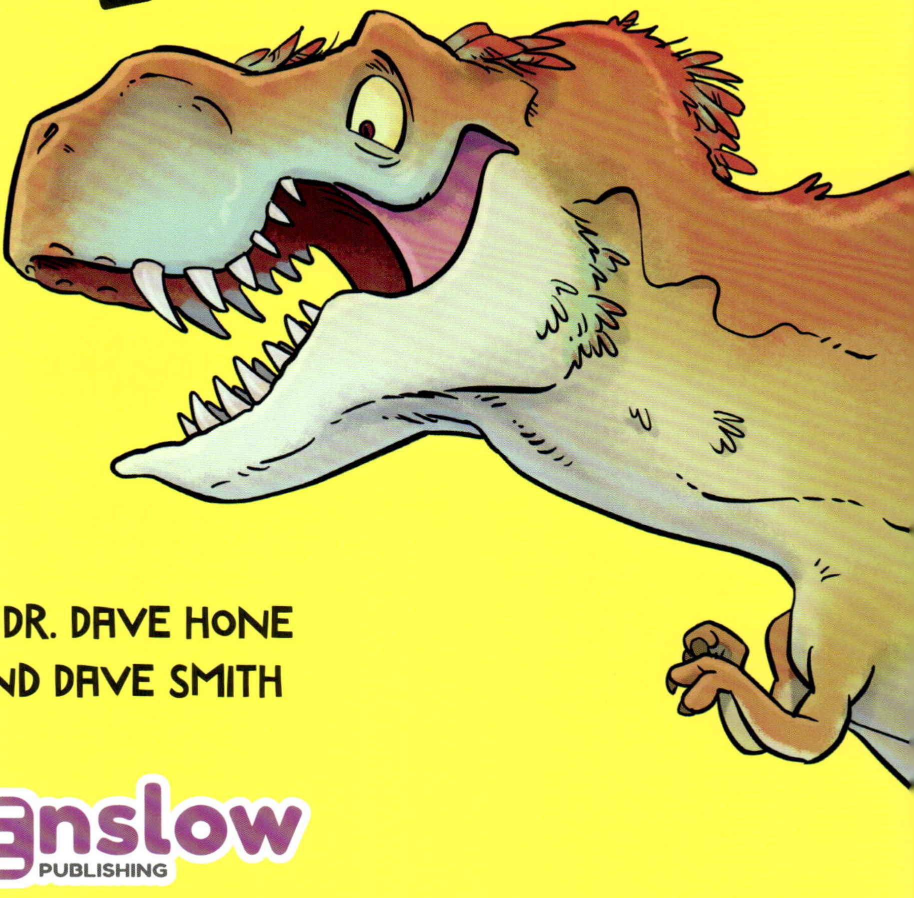

BY DR. DAVE HONE
AND DAVE SMITH

Enslow
PUBLISHING

Published in 2026 by Enslow Publishing, LLC
2544 Clinton Street
Buffalo, NY 14224

First published in Great Britain in 2023 by Wayland
Copyright © Hodder and Stoughton, 2023
All rights reserved

Editors: Christina Webb and Elise Short
Design: Emma DeBanks

The website addresses (URLs) included in this book were valid at the time of going to press. However, it is possible that contents or addresses may have changed since the publication of this book.

No responsibility for any such changes can be accepted by either the author or the Publisher.

All rights reserved. No part of this book may be reproduced in any form without permission in writing from the publisher, except by a reviewer.

Printed in China

CPSIA compliance information: Batch #QW26ENS: For further information contact Enslow Publishing LLC, New York, New York at 1-800-398-2504.

Please visit our website, www.enslowpublishing.com. For a free color catalog of all our high-quality books, call toll free 1-800-398-2504 or fax 1-877-980-4454.

Cataloging-in-Publication Data
Names: Hone, David (Paleontologist), author. | Smith, Dave, illustrator.
Title: Whose bum did T. rex bite? / by Dr. Dave Hone, illustrated by Dave Smith.
Description: Buffalo, NY : Enslow Publishing, 2026. | Series: Dinosaur science | Includes glossary and index.
Identifiers: ISBN 9781978547315 (pbk.) | ISBN 9781978547322 (library bound) | ISBN 9781978547339 (ebook)
Subjects: LCSH: Dinosaurs--Juvenile literature. | Dinosaurs--Food--Juvenile literature. | Reptiles, Fossil--Juvenile literature. | Extinct reptiles--Juvenile literature. | Paleontology--Juvenile literature.
Classification: LCC QE862.D5 H66 2026 | DDC 567.9--dc23

Find us on

CONTENTS

What Did Dinosaurs Eat? 4
What They Left Behind.................................. 6
Many, Many Meat Eaters 8
A Mega-Long Poo 10
Not Quite Eaten... 12
Finding Snacks 14
What Else Lurks Inside?.............................. 16
Fishy Business 18
Mega Plant Eaters...................................... 20
The Biggest Poo, Number 2......................... 22
Beaks and Teeth... 24
The Duck-billed Dinosaurs 26
What We Don't Know 28
Glossary... 30
Further information..................................... 31
Index 32

WHAT DID DINOSAURS EAT?

Dinosaurs roamed Earth for over 150 million years. From rainforests to deserts to coasts, they lived in every kind of habitat on every continent. So it shouldn't be a surprise to learn that between them they ate all kinds of different foods.

Different Diets

Some dinosaurs ate plants: the herbivores. Some were meat eaters: the carnivores. And the omnivores ate both plants and meat.

How do we Know?

How can paleontologists (dinosaur scientists) work out what dinosaurs ate when they have been dead for 65 million years?

One way is to study fossils. Fossils are the remains or traces of once-living things that have turned to stone over time. Even poo can turn into a fossil. Fossils can help scientists figure out what dinosaurs ate and how they ate it.

Paleontologists also look for clues in the shapes of dinosaur teeth and jaws and in bite marks on bones. They sometimes even find the remains of a dinosaur's last meal preserved inside its fossilized skeleton.

WHAT THEY LEFT BEHIND

It's actually quite rare for fossils to form. Usually when a living thing dies it is either eaten by other living things or it rots away leaving nothing behind. But when the conditions are just right, they fossilize.

The Perfect Storm

For a fossil to form, the process of rotting away needs to be stopped. This happens when the remains of an organism are suddenly buried and covered over in a flood, landslide, or sandstorm, for example.

1. Caught in a sudden sandstorm, this dinosaur will not become someone else's meal.

2. Layers of sand and soil build up and bury the remains deep underground.

DID YOU KNOW?

It's not just the remains of living things that can become fossils, but their activities and behaviors, too. Things like footprints, poo, nests, and burrows can also be preserved and these are called trace fossils.

4. Rivers and weather wear away rock, slowly revealing the fossil.

3. The chemicals from tiny bits of rock called sediments work their way into the bones and slowly transform them into stone. This process takes millions of years.

The Harder the Better

The most common fossils are made from hard body parts such as bones, teeth, and shells as they take longer to rot away. Softer body parts such as skin, muscles, organs, and even eggs, can fossilize too, but these are much rarer as they decompose much faster.

MANY, MANY MEAT EATERS

Scientists have now named over 500 species of carnivorous (meat-eating) dinosaurs. They vary enormously in shape and size, from little 20-inch (50-cm) beasts the size of a crow to 40-foot (12-m) giants like *Tyrannosaurus rex* (*T. rex*).

Dinner-Catching Tools

Most meat-eating animals today – whether birds, mammals, or reptiles – have similar features to help them catch and eat their dinner.

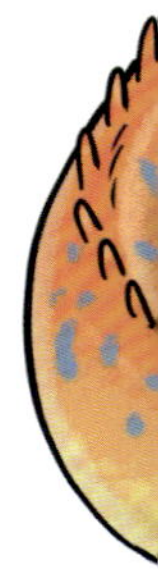

DID YOU KNOW?

All carnivorous dinosaurs are part of a group called the theropods. But some of them, such as the Therizinosaurus, dropped meat from their diet and changed to eating plants.

Carnivorous dinosaurs had many similar features to the predators of today.

A MEGA-LONG POO

Guess how big the poo of a giant 40-foot (12-m) long *T. rex* was? Paleontologists discovered a fossilized *T. rex* poo in southern Saskatchewan in Canada that was over 3 feet (1 m) long. Imagine how that would have smelled! It was also a bit, well, splattery (before it dried and was fossilized). Perhaps the owner wasn't well before it did its business.

Baby duck-billed dinosaur

What's in the Poo?

The *T. rex*'s fossilized poo is full of tiny bits of the bones of a baby duck-billed dinosaur. So we know from this amazing fossil poo that *T. rex* was eating baby dinosaurs.

Paleontologists have found teeth, claws, scales, bits of shell, and seeds in fossilized poo. They also noticed signs of dung beetles burrowing through the poo. A fossilized poo reveals lots of information about what a dinosaur ate but also what other animals lived alongside it.

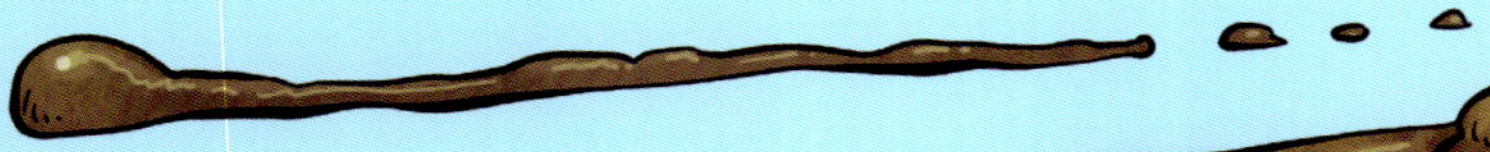

DID YOU KNOW?

A fossilized poo is called a coprolite. It's not just dinosaur coprolites that have been found. The fossilized poos of ancient turtles, sharks, and mammals have been discovered too!

NOT QUITE EATEN

Carnivores don't manage to make a meal of every animal they set their eyes on. Most of the time they aren't able to sneak up on or grab what they are after, but it might be a close call ...

Toothy Trophy

Paleontologists found the bones of an *Edmontosaurus* with *T. rex* teeth stuck in them. Ouch! The teeth would have broken off when the predator tried to stop its dinner from escaping.

Not only that, but the *Edmontosaurus*'s bones had healed and new bone had grown over the tooth. It lived to walk away with tiny bits of *T. rex* in its body. Imagine if you had a lion's tooth stuck inside you!

Bum Injuries

The injuries we see on these intended meals were on their bums, legs, or tail – tyrannosaurs were trying to bite their prey on the bum as they ran away!

FINDING SNACKS

Carnivores don't just eat things they've killed. They also eat animals that died of old age, illness, or from an accident. Feeding on animals that are already dead is called scavenging. Yuck!

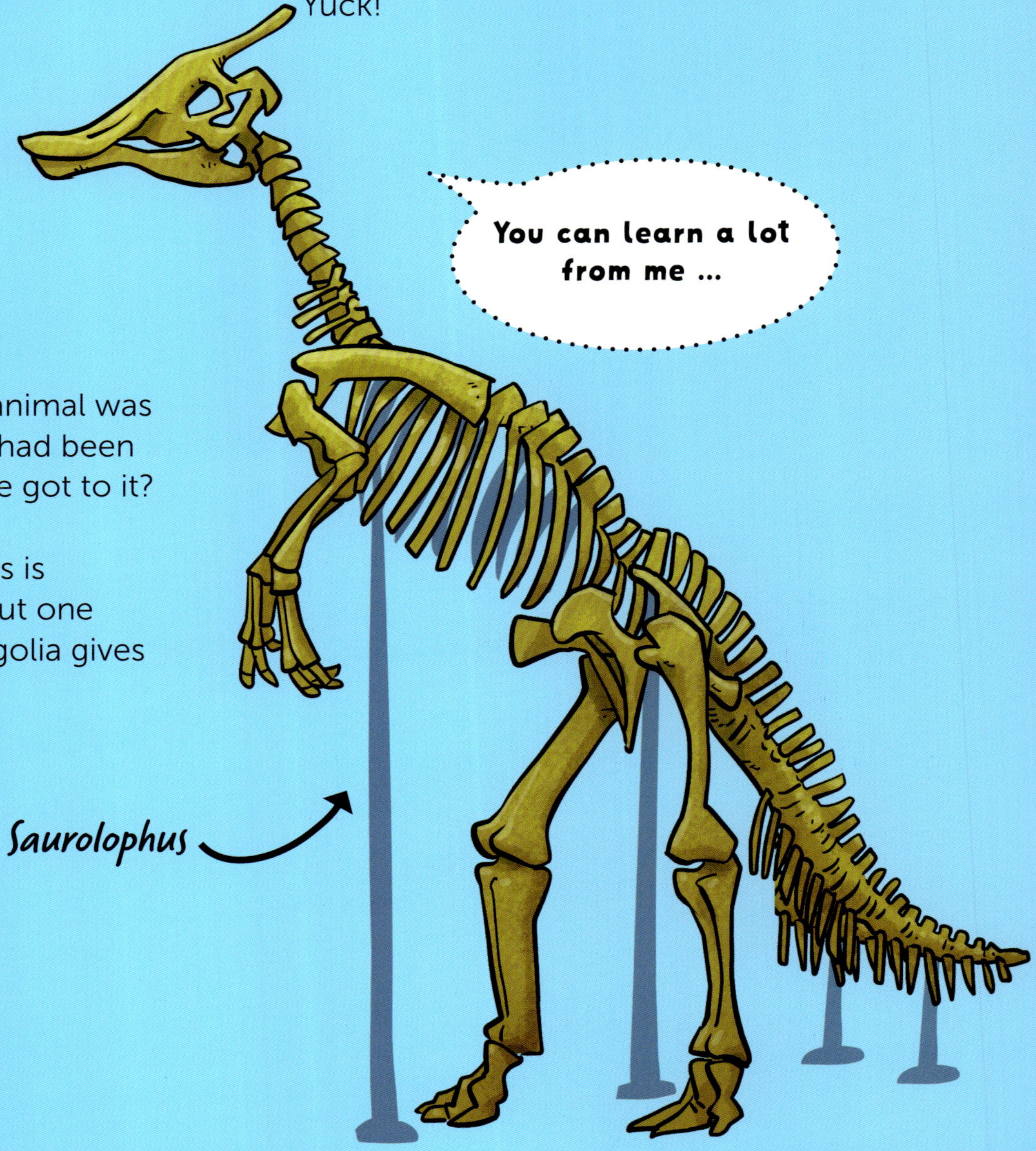

Detective Work

How can we know if an animal was killed and then eaten, or had been dead before the carnivore got to it?

Detecting this from fossils is obviously very difficult. But one such skeleton from Mongolia gives us a good answer.

River Dinner

The fossilized bones of a large herbivore called *Saurolophus* were found in rock where an ancient river once ran. Its bones show damage from the river and one arm is covered in bite marks from a big tyrannosaur. These bites are on top of the damage from the river, so the *Saurolophus* must already have been dead when the tyrannosaur had a nibble.

DID YOU KNOW?

Tyrannosaurs were rather neat and effective eaters. They used different teeth for different tasks. The tyrannosaur that found the *Saurolophus* bit hard with its biggest teeth to try and rip the herbivore's arm off. Then it used its small front teeth to scrape the flesh off the bone.

WHAT ELSE LURKS INSIDE?

Sometimes paleontologists get lucky. They find fossilized dinosaurs with their last meal fossilized inside them. These finds provide lots of invaluable information about dinosaur diets as well as the other creatures that lived alongside them.

Not a Fussy Eater

Small carnivores had a huge range of foods they could feast on. Three fossilized *Microraptor* skeletons – small, feathered dinosaurs – were found in China with three different animals' bones inside them. One ate some fish, one ate the foot of a mammal, and one had a whole bird inside it! Clearly these dinosaurs would eat anything. Who knows what else they might have gobbled up?

Insides Preserved

The even smaller fossilized *Scipionyx*, found in Italy, actually has the shape of its stomach and intestines preserved. In the guts of this long-dead dinosaur we can see the bones of a lizard and many bones and scales from small fish.

Wing-swallower

A *Velociraptor* fossil has been discovered with part of a very long pterosaur wing bone inside it. Eating this must have required a trick like sword-swallowing to get it down!

FISHY BUSINESS

Fish make tasty meals, but they are very slippery and hard to catch. Thanks to some particular features, one group of dinosaurs were perhaps better at catching fish than any other – the spinosaurs.

Splashing Around

The spinosaur group includes some of the largest land-living carnivores of all time. They are famous for having a sail on their back, giant claws on their hands, and crocodile-like snouts. Spinosaurs are thought to have fished like herons and storks with their snout just below the water, jabbing their head down to grab at fish.

Grab and Snap

We know that they ate fish because a fossilized *Baryonyx,* a British spinosaur, was found with fossilized fish scales still in its belly. But just like today's crocodiles, they used their long, narrow, powerful jaws to grab and snap at other creatures, too. The *Baryonyx* hadn't just eaten fish for its dinner – it also had a baby dinosaur's bones in its stomach. Greedy!

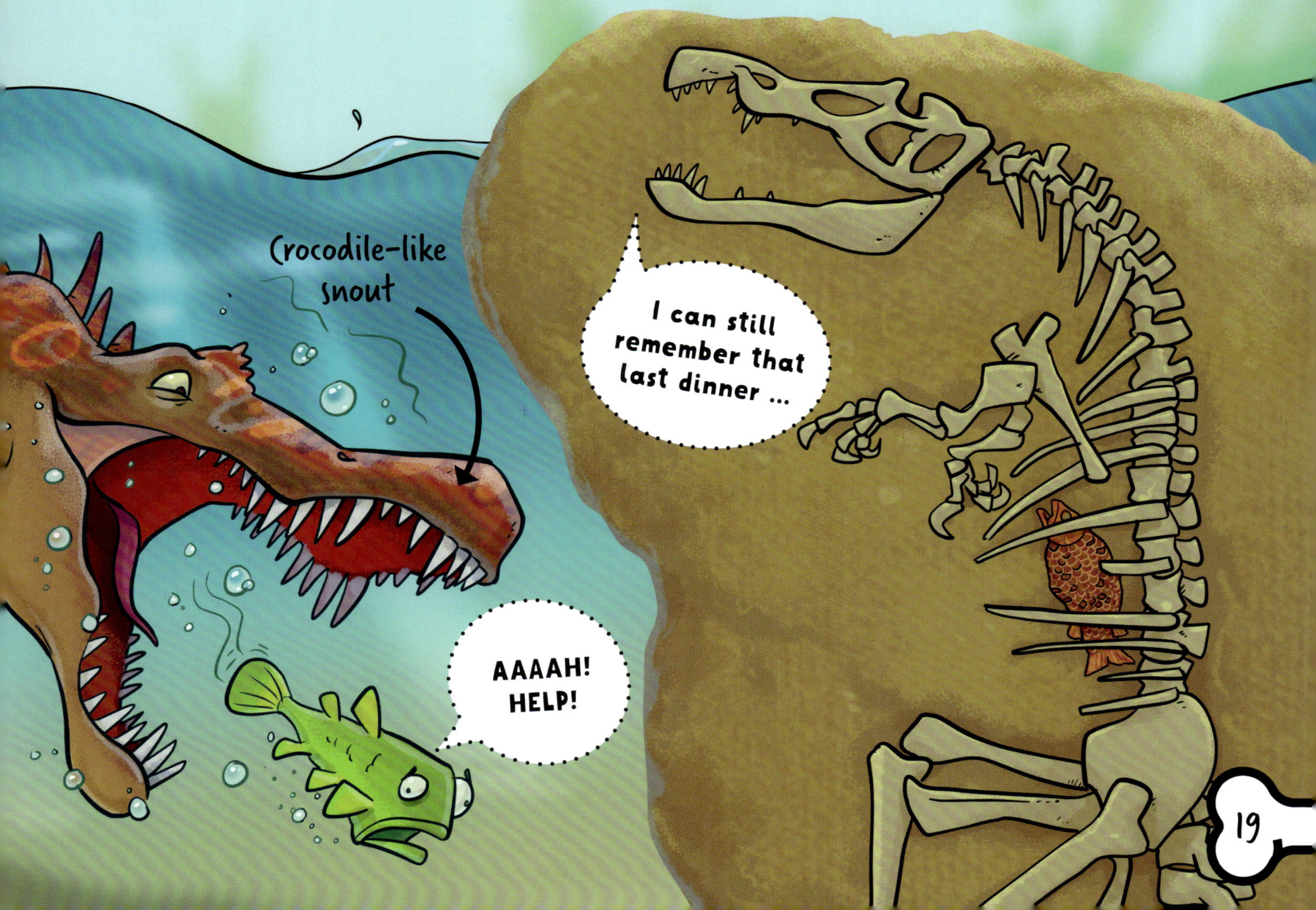

MEGA PLANT EATERS

The largest dinosaurs belong to a group called the sauropods. They are famous not only for being big, but for having long necks supporting tiny heads, and often very long tails. The sauropods ate plants.

The largest sauropods could weigh up to 55 tons (50 mt): about the same as a herd of 15 elephants!

Always Hungry

Animals this big need A LOT of food, so sauropods were always on the move to find enough plants to keep them going. Imagine walking and eating for 12 hours a day or more!

DID YOU KNOW?

Sauropods had very simple teeth and most of them just grabbed any plants they could, bit them off and swallowed them down. As they didn't chew, they needed a very large digestive system to break down their food. This may explain why they were so big.

Dino Vacuums

Sauropods didn't have time to chew or be choosy. Their long necks would help them reach up into trees or sweep across the ground to access as many plants as possible without having to move far. When you're that big, walking is an effort!

THE BIGGEST POO, NUMBER 2

The biggest dinosaurs were a group of sauropods called the titanosaurs. Many of them, including the largest ones, came from South America, but they lived in many other places too, including India. Some of the Indian titanosaurs left behind more than just fossil skeletons.

Huge Poos

Paleontologists have found fossilized titanosaur poo. This is actually really rare. If you think of a carnivore's poo, it is more likely to fossilize because it contains hard bits of bone that can be preserved. A herbivore's poo, however, is made up of the remains of twigs and leaves, which rot and break down faster than bone. So their squishy poos are less likely to become fossils.

High or Low

Few plant-eater poos have been found, but the ones that we have are HUGE! They have given us clues to what titanosaurs ate: bits of grasses and some flowering plants but very little traces of trees. This tells us that these giant dinosaurs were mostly feeding low down and not reaching up for food, high in the trees, like some other sauropods.

BEAKS AND TEETH

The sauropods were not the only plant-eating dinosaurs. A diverse group of animals called the ornithischians were also herbivores. They came in all shapes and sizes, from stegosaurs with their plates, to ceratopsians with their horns, and the thick-headed pachycephalosaurs. But they all had the same beak and teeth arrangement.

Beak-breaking Business

The ornithischians had an unusual combination of beak and teeth. Fossil finds have shown that the beak at the front of their mouth was used to cut up tough plants. The plants were then ground down by the teeth in their jaws before being swallowed.

Chew, Chew, Chew

Breaking food down before swallowing it is a great way to help start the digestion process. It makes it easier for the body to take out all the useful energy-making parts of the food. Being able to chew the plants they ate meant that the ornithischians didn't need to be as huge as the sauropods to be efficient eaters (see page 20).

THE DUCK-BILLED DINOSAURS

One group of ornithischians, the hadrosaurs, had sharp beaks that were good for cutting food. Inside their beaks were rows and rows of teeth to help them chew their food. They ate tough plants that wore their teeth away quickly, so they were always growing new ones in order to keep eating.

DID YOU KNOW?

Hadrosaurs could have over 1,000 teeth at a time – just imagine the dentist bill if something went wrong with them!

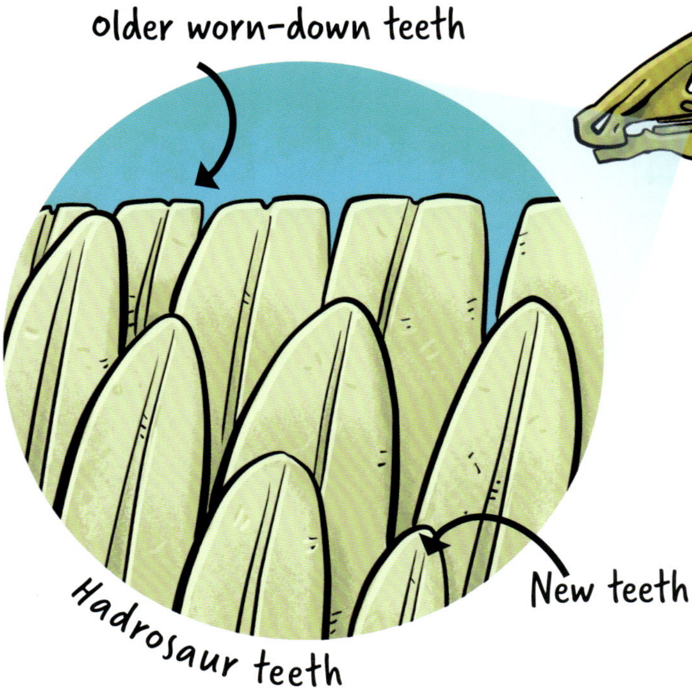

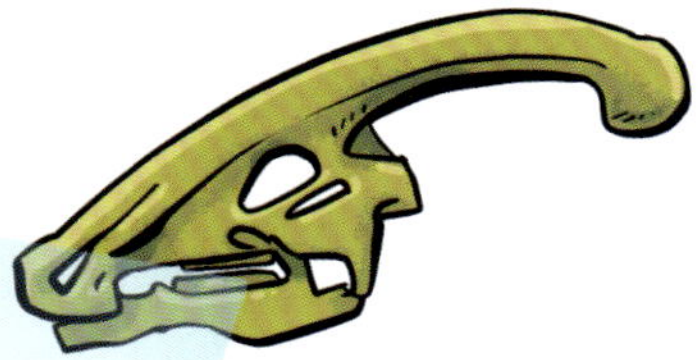

Chewing Machine

Hadrosaurs were impressive chewing machines. Unlike other dinosaurs, they did not lose their teeth: they just grew new ones next to the worn-down ones. A hadrosaur's mouth could contain many stacks of six or more teeth side by side!

Herbivore or Carnivore?

We know the hadrosaurs ate plants because some hadrosaur fossil skeletons had bits of leaves still preserved inside them. Their fossilized poo revealed that among bits of wood, there were pieces of clam shell! But scientists don't think they were actually hunting for shellfish – these clams were probably living on dead wood in a pond and the hadrosaurs ate them by accident.

WHAT WE DON'T KNOW

Even though dinosaurs have been dead for 65 million years, it is amazing how much information paleontologists can work out about what they ate and how.

We still have a lot to learn about dinosaur diets. Here are some animals that have left scientists confused. Maybe one day you can help solve the mystery of their diet.

Limusaurus inextricibalis

An adult *Limusaurus* had a beak and, like chickens, swallowed stones to help break up seeds in its stomach. When it was young, it had teeth, no beak, and no stomach stones. So what was it eating?

Fossil finds of *Limusaurus* at different stages of its life cycle show that it lost its teeth as it grew up but didn't grow any more. Instead it formed a beak. Because the baby's teeth were sharp enough to be able to eat meat, this change in features is thought to indicate a change in diet as it grew: from eating insects and other small animals to plants.

Oviraptor

This dinosaur had strong claws on its hands, a sharp beak and no teeth. Did it use its beak to kill prey or for cutting sharp vegetation? We still haven't figured it out. It might have been doing both.

Pelecanimimus

This carnivorous dinosaur had lots of small teeth and a big throat pouch like a pelican. It might have been gulping down fish or it could have been a filter feeder, like a flamingo, filtering out tiny bits of food from water.

GLOSSARY

Coprolite – a fossilized poo or dropping.

Decompose – to become rotten and break down into little pieces.

Diet – the kinds of food that a person or animal usually eats.

Dinosaur – one of a group of extinct reptiles that were the dominant land animals from around 225-65 million years ago. Their descendants live on today – birds.

Flood – a large amount of water covering an area that is usually dry.

Fossil – the remains of an ancient animal or plant (or remains from their movements, such as footprints) that have turned to stone.

Herbivore – an animal that mostly or entirely eats plants.

Landslide – rock and earth moving suddenly and quickly down a mountain.

Life cycle – the series of changes that a living thing goes through from the beginning of its life until death.

Omnivore – an animal that eats plants and animals.

Organ – a part of the body of an animal or plant that performs a particular job, such as the heart.

Ornithischian – one of a group of plant-eating dinosaurs. Some walked on two legs and others on four, and many of them had armor or head crests with spikes on them.

Predator – an animal that mostly or entirely eats meat (including things like fish, eggs, and insects).

Pterosaur – one of a group of ancient flying reptiles that lived alongside their close relatives, the dinosaurs.

Sandstorm – a strong wind in a desert carrying a large amount of sand.

Sauropod – one of a group of dinosaurs that were large in size, with long necks and tails. They walked on four legs and ate plants.

Scavenger – an animal that mostly or entirely eats animals that are already dead.

Species – a set of animals or plants that have similar characteristics to each other.

Theropod – one of a group of meat-eating dinosaurs (though some switched and ate plants) that walked on two legs.

FURTHER INFORMATION

Books
Body Bits: Dead-awesome Dinosaur Body Facts by Paul Mason and Dave Smith (Wayland, 2021)

Dinosaur Infosaurus series by Katie Woolley (Wayland, 2021)

Dino-Sorted series by Sonya Newland and Izzi Howell (Gareth Stevens Publishing, 2026)

Websites
Find out about dinosaurs and prehistoric life:
kids.nationalgeographic.com/animals/prehistoric

Watch a video explaining how paleontologists find clues about what dinosaurs and other extinct animals ate:
naturalhistory.si.edu/education/teaching-resources/paleontology/how-do-we-know-what-dinosaurs-and-other-extinct-animals

Explore the Natural History Museum's directory of dinosaurs:
www.nhm.ac.uk/discover/dino-directory.html

Play games, watch videos, and learn about palaeontology:
www.amnh.org/explore/ology/paleontology

INDEX

beaks 24, 26, 28–29
beetles, dung 10–11
bones 5, 7, 10, 12, 15–17, 19, 22

carnivores 4, 8–19, 22, 27–29
ceratopsians 24
coprolites 11 (see also poos)

dinosaur (species)
- *Baryonyx* 19
- *Diplodocus* 23
- *Edmontosaurus* 12–13
- *Limusaurus* 28
- *Microraptor* 16
- *Oviraptor* 29
- *Pelecanimimus* 29
- *Saurolophus* 14–15
- *Scipionyx* 17
- *Therizinosaurus* 9
- *Tyrannosaurus rex* (*T. rex*) 8–13, 15
- *Velociraptor* 17

fish 5, 16–19, 29
fossils 5–7, 10–17, 19, 22–24, 27–28
- how fossils form 6–7

hadrosaurs 26–27
herbivores 4, 9, 15, 20–29

jaws 5, 8–9, 24

omnivores 4
ornithischians 24–27

pachycephalosaurs 24
paleontologists 5, 10, 12, 16, 22, 28
paleoscatologists 11
poos 5, 7, 10–11, 22–23, 27
pterosaurs 17

sauropods 20–25
shells 7, 10, 27
spinosaurs 18–19
stegosaurs 24

teeth 5, 7–10, 12, 15, 21, 24, 26–29
theropods 9
titanosaurs 22–23
tyrannosaurs 12–13, 15 (see also *T. rex*)